Teilhard de Chardin
on
Love and Suffering

Teilhard de Chardin
on
Love and Suffering

by
Paul Chauchard

Translated by

Marie Chêne

DEUS BOOKS
PAULIST PRESS
(Paulist Fathers)
Glen Rock, New Jersey

A Deus Books Edition of the Paulist Press, 1966, by special arrangement with Éditions Universitaires, Paris, France.

Nihil Obstat: William F. Hogan, S.T.D.
Censor Librorum

Imprimatur: ✠ Thomas A. Boland, S.T.D.
Archbishop of Newark
May 20, 1966

Cover Design: Claude Ponsot
Published by Paulist Press
Editorial Office: 304 W. 58th St., N.Y., N. Y. 10019
Business Office: Glen Rock, New Jersey 07452

Manufactured in the
United States of America

Contents

PART ONE

Teilhard de Chardin
The Witness of Love

PART TWO

Teilhard de Chardin
and the
Optimism of the Cross

5

6   *Contents*

PART ONE
Teilhard de Chardin
The Witness of Love

Let us only believe. May we believe the harder and the more despairingly as reality seems the more threatening and irreducible. And then little by little we shall see the universal horror relax, and smile at us, and enfold us in more-than-human arms.

THE DIVINE MILIEU

I
Misunderstood
and Needed

Recently, Titov and Gagarin announced that they had seen no sign of God, angels, or paradise on their flight through space. Soon after, the Marxists declared that matter, whose inexhaustible power they celebrate, is radically absurd; and Jean Paul Sartre humorously reproached them for such a logic-defying dismissal of theology. Now we hear Garaudy and Kahane inform us that to understand the world scientifically, atheist rationalists need none other than a Jesuit priest, known for his authentic Christian faith. They say that they agree with him on the necessity for historical analysis of nature which—to them—proves the uselessness of God.

Yet the thought of Father Teilhard de Chardin could not be more misunderstood than by thus viewing God's place in it as only a useless superstructure. For Teilhard, what is essential is not the historical analysis of nature. It is rather that such analysis, sometimes claimed as atheistic, necessarily leads the reason not to agnosticism, or vague religious sentiments, or to dim notions of a marginal God for philosophers and scholars, but straight to mystic encounter with

Jesus Christ, the God of love. Teilhard is neither a
scientist who happens to be a believer nor a priest
with a side career in scientific research. He is a
whole man, in no way divided by his doubled research and doubled experience in the objective science of matter and in the knowledge of God. To try
to split him into a man of science and a man of faith
is to fail to understand him, even if one seems to agree
with his evolutionary views or if one were of the same
religion as he. Until he died on the feast of the Resurrection, a day which proclaims the glorious secret of
matter to mankind, he gave himself unstintingly to
his work. And his work was precisely that of reinsert-
ing Christianity in the world, in the spirit of the
Bible, St. John, St. Paul, the Fathers and St. Thomas
Aquinas, with an "optimism" convinced that nothing
else could turn the world aside from self-destruction.
Humanity is as much in danger from the opium of a
disincarnate religion, which could not be that of
Christ, as from the new opium of a science which denies the spirit its full dimensions.

No one understands this better than President Sen-
ghor of Senegal. He has told us how tempting Marxism
with its technical efficiency was for Negro intellectuals, who might have endangered the mystic soul
of Africa thereby; and how Teilhard delivered them
from it by giving back to technical effort its sacred
dimension which safeguards the human person.
"Lacking the infusion of new physical blood," Teilhard tells us, "Christian spirituality risks weakening
itself and getting lost in the clouds. And, lacking
infusion of a principle of universal love, man's sense
of progress even more certainly risks turning away hor-
rified from the frightening cosmic machine with
which it finds itself engaged."

Even in childhood in the Auvergne mountains,
young Pierre had two interests, two passionate call-

ings. One was for nature, rocks and stones; but he realized with grief that they could offer him only the contingent and the ephemeral. He knew where the Absolute lay, that order of love celebrated by an earlier Christian scientist, his compatriot Pascal who led him toward his religious vocation. It would have been easy for him to forget the rocks for God and just as easy to forget God for the rocks; it would have been simpler still to cut himself in two, as a good priest with an interest in the natural sciences.

The originality of Teilhard, the providential secret which made him the indispensable prophet of the modern world, was his surety that we need not turn away from the world, the contingent, the many in order to meet God the Absolute. There is no need to search for God beyond the remote beyond; he is hidden but discoverable right at the heart of matter. Though a godless cosmonaut finds support in the enthusiasm of his countrymen, the immensities of infinite space no longer chill us; we inhabit, "in its evolution, a universe charged with love" which mankind can cherish. The scientist need no longer lose himself in the superficial excitement of phenomena. His task is to understand the secret meaning of the phenomena that beings manifest, "the inwardness of things" that leads us right to their Creator. Therein may lie the realization that the true end of scientific activity is to bring us to God, not by a false dismissal of distinctions—for God is spirit and by definition outside the scope of material science, one proof of which may well be scientific atheism—but because the scientific discovery of the meaning of the universe leads logically to God.

In areas where matter and spirit, science and faith, the laboratory and the oratory are customarily kept well apart, Teilhard certainly does nothing to confuse their boundaries. He shows us not that separate fields can be united but that it is possible to entertain two different points of view of a single reality. He replaces the inverse errors of false unity and false disparity with the truth of concordance and convergence. He had a most sensible kind of prudence and an experimenter's skepticism. For him, the understanding of faith then became his hypothesis about the world; he sought not to demonstrate it completely but to find the beginnings of its confirmation by science. If it were true, then science, losing nothing of the nature proper to it, would find its scope extended to the furthest extremes. Faith is then like an airplane which enables us to sight under a field traces of a Roman ruin which from a ground view might objectively and in good faith be denied. The method works both ways. This Christian faith, which has just shown how it can make the scientist a better scientist despite the usual prejudice to the contrary, is often seen as a supernatural thing just as useless as it is distant from earthly reality. Once we understand the meaning of matter, we must restore to Christianity, the religion of God the Creator and Savior, its meaning as the religion of matter and of history. To do so does not mean "changing religion around", altering the Catholic dogmas modern rationalism commonly attacks. It means on the contrary understanding these dogmas in their strictest orthodoxy and stripping our views of them of heresy, for science's sake.

Scientific atheism busily proves to us that God has no beard and no hands; that there is no Ancient Architect of the Universe; that mature adults do not need the sentimental God of Victorian novels. None of these notions coincide with the Catholic concept of God, which the atheistic arguments only serve to make more clear. Possibly, however, the clarity is apparent only to one who has already met the true God through faith. If Teilhard could so readily find

God in matter, it was because he already knew God through faith. Although unquestionably objective and scientific, the work of Teilhard is that of a believer.

His work has as a substructure belief in the eucharist, a belief that induces the habit of seeing within accidental things the profoundest reality, the real presence. When Teilhard takes us by the hand, he leads us step by step from pure analytic science to Catholic theology's loftiest mystic understanding of God. He shows us that he does not pervert the facts to do so but that he is faithful to the vision of reality allowed him by his path which he did not foresee. And all the time he is well aware that he is not putting God on exhibit, nor offering us a painless, effortless faith and a platterful of proofs. "You're lucky to have your faith!" say some unbelievers; because faith is a mystery of grace, they falsely conclude that it is achieved without effort and thought. It is this effort, this thought, that Teilhard suggests to us in making us witnesses of his vision. He shows unbelievers how tempting, how interesting, is that Catholic vision which they had found outdated and unrelated to the modern world. What use is the redemption to the descendant of Picanthropus who is getting ready for his trip to the moon? That is the question! Teilhard also makes science religiously relevant to the believers who thought it a diabolic attempt to wipe out the sense of the sacred and who had sought spiritual salvation in despising the goods of this world.

Teilhard knows how to belong to both worlds which think that, because they speak different languages and are ignorant of each other, they are enemies. This ability of his is denied by a fair number of his specialized readers, be they scientists, philosophers or theologians. The scientist does not recognize himself in the Teilhardian view; he accuses Teilhard of supplying atoms with a loving soul, then re-

proaches him with completely abandoning positive
scientific objectivity for reasons of false apologetics.
He sees in this visionary a philosopher, a poet and a
prophet—qualities which are, sad to say, not praise
in the mouth of a scientist.

The philosopher in turn notes that the Teilhardian
synthesis appears in his usual field; not finding it to
be what he usually calls philosophy, he then says
that Teilhard—despite his denials—was in fact talking
philosophy, but bad philosophy, into which he was
dragged powerless, probably by the demands of his
faith, as soon as he left the field of analytic science.
Finally, there is the accusation that he was a material-
ist, since he agrees with the materialists in celebrat-
ing the spiritualizing capacities of matter. Along come
the traditional theologians, who wax indignant and
declare that Teilhard's theology is a grave deformation of Catholic faith; while their joyous opponents
claim that Teilhard has contributed the new religion
of a new era.

Experience thus shows that in spite of all his pre-
cautions, Teilhard is so new (like St. Paul!) that he
does not entirely succeed in making himself understood. It is therefore necessary to explain him. Teilhard is in no sense a new St. Thomas come to give
us a summation of science and faith that would ren-
der further effort unnecessary. He obliges us to think
and to understand the total meaning of the world.
Teilhard is a paleontologist and a believer. In the
convergence of the meaning of evolution and of his
Catholic faith, he offers us a perspective, a point of
reference for understanding the world, its future and
the duty of mankind. He does not try to be complete,
to finish off the work of every other scientist, to explain the inner laws of atoms to physicists, to take
over the tasks of sociologists, economists and his-

torians, or to give us a complete set of formulas for every dogma.

His special field lay in two directions. In one, he showed us that science cannot restrict itself to the level of analysis but should, without becoming a philosophy, give us an overall, coherent, meaningful view of the world and objectively set man in the place suited to his subjectivity. In the other, he recalls that Christian dogmas, if essentially supernatural, are yet not disincarnate and do take nature into account. So, if we hope to find in Teilhard a catechism or a complete theology, we shall be disappointed and inclined to accuse him of misrepresenting dogma. Against such accusations, however, we need no longer defend him, since the brilliant studies of his work by Father Wildiers and Father de Lubac have amply demonstrated the sorry weakness of his opponents' arguments.

Teilhard's twofold mission was to establish the superstructures of science, as a scientist, and to explore the inner structures of faith, as a believer. He built thereby a two-way, two-level bridge over the gaping abyss that cut science off from faith and made them seem hostile strangers.

We might examine all of Teilhard's work, to show this span between an authentic science (that of tomorrow rather than yesterday, whence its heuristic value in the development of research) and an authentic Catholicism, freed of every trace of Manicheanism, Jansenism and naturalistic Pelagianism. However, we shall here consider simply the essential, the high point of Teilhard's thought: the problem of *love*. How a scientist should investigate love—there's a question that by definition defies scientific objectivity! Either love is a value of another order entirely, pertinent only to human spirituality, or it is camouflage for a base, anti-rational sentimentality which enables women to accept the erotic realities! We would be willing to hear Freud speak as a biologist about love. We would be willing to hear fine sermons on God who is love. But we don't expect both served up in one dish!

Paradoxically, the best way to make Teilhard understood is by not talking about him, by not commenting on him; it is better to quote from his work. It is Teilhard himself who must be read, but read with confidence in his scientific veracity and his Catholic orthodoxy. Then let us see if science is or is not able to arrive at love hidden in the world and if that love might lead logically to the Catholic faith. Some reproach Teilhard's followers with being blinded by adoration. May I suggest that what I have to offer to Teilhardian critique does not rise from a leader-follower relationship. It lies in the fact that I am, like Teilhard, a biologist, more exactly, a neurophysiologist and therefore at least apparently very material-minded. Further, I am, like him, a Catholic, though a convert, whose conversion brought not the least rejection of the truths of seemingly materialistic science but did force me to philosophical reflection aimed at understanding the true meaning of matter.

Conceivably, the physicist of inanimate matter or the psychologist of behavior can separate faith and science without too much trouble. No such possibility is open to the neurophysiologist of the human brain or the paleontologist of man's evolutionary origins. Starting from this personal experience, I can confirm and complete the work of unification Teilhard did, starting from paleontology. Does science objectively encounter love? Yes, it does, as we shall see; it is possible to develop a biology and a neurophysiology of love (agapology). Quite objectively, the golden rule of individual and social mental balance is, "Love your neighbor as yourself", in reference to a higher love, of which the perfect form is the personal love of a personal God who is love.

II

Degrees of Amorization:
A Review of Agapology

"Usually we think of love (and with what analytic refinement!) only in its sentimental aspect: the joys and pains it causes us. It is in its natural dynamism and its evolutionary significance that I find myself led to examine it here, in order to determine the ultimate phases of the phenomenon of man. Considered in its full biological reality, love (that is, the affinity of being for being) is not particular to man. It stands for a general property of all life, and as such it espouses in their varieties and degrees all the forms successively taken by organized matter. Among the mammals, who are quite close to us, we readily recognize it with its diverse modalities: sexual passion, paternal or maternal instinct, social solidarity, etc. Further, or lower, on the Tree of Life, the analogies are less clear. They thin out almost to invisibility. . . . But . . . if some internal propulsion toward union did not exist even in a state undoubtedly most rudimentary yet already being born, it would be physically impossible for love to appear at a higher level, among us, in the state of having become man. Under the propulsion of love, it is the fragments of the world which search for each other in order that the world may come into being. . . . Love in all its nuances is nothing other and nothing less than the more or less direct impression marked on the heart of the element by the psychic convergence of the universe upon itself."

Teilhard sets forth clearly a fundamental law, starting from the phenomenology of biological evolution (not from theories of its mechanisms or its metaphysics but from the *fact* of the chronological succession of fossils). That is, that evolution is neither as absurd nor as incoherent as it looks to those who analyze it only in its details. It has a meaning that consists of the appearance of beings which are more and more complex, the degree of complexity being in some way measured by the progress of the organ of individual organization, behavior, and intelligent mastery, the brain. Since it is *ascent toward the greatest brain,* which is the human brain, evolution is also the ascent of psychism, of consciousness and of freedom. The more organization progresses, and the more inadequate a classic presentation of outward appearance becomes, the more urgent it is to take into account the *inwardness of things.* First, and objectively, this inwardness consists of complexity in interior organization; but further, through the brain, this same interior is responsible for the degree of psychological *interiority* and self-mastery.

This does not mean endowing stones with human consciousness. It simply means seeing that between the simplest inanimate objects and the most complex living things there is an unbroken chain in which the constant factor is the existence of an organization, a force imposed on simple, frequently changing elements, and in which what progresses is complexity of organization. The degree of consciousness is measured by the degree of development of the brain.

Having the most complex brain capable of interior language, man has crossed *the threshold of reflection*. That he may seem objectively to modern psychology to have a psyche of an entirely different order in no way implies separating man radically from the animal by denying the parallel rise of psychism, consciousness and brain from amoeba to man. The amoeba, with no brain, is also indebted to its psychism which, though abridged and inferior, already contains in a germinal state everything that will open out, due to the brain, in a superior being. It owes its psychism to the fact that it is not a chance juxtaposition of molecules but a small individual acting as a whole, therefore a small presence in the world, a microinteriority apt at self-defense.

The biologist who cannot take interest (as Claude Bernard has so clearly seen) only in the analytic aspect of living things, their organs and functions, but must keep in mind the unity of the being in a synthetic view, asking himself how the parts work for the welfare of the whole, cannot conceive of science as does the physicist who contents himself with observing phenomena. One might be an excellent paleontologist and contribute to the progress of science through being a specialist in this or that organ of some particular group, period and country. Under such conditions, the facts observed—which are the sole basis of scientific progress—may be so insignificant that one might conclude from them that the transformations of life are absurd. The paleontologist has not fully reached the potential extent of his profession until he takes a longer view and sees appear, despite the incoherence of details, the great, meaningful sequences. It was at one time possible to believe it scientifically correct to deny the superiority of man, which today is a plain scientific fact, incontestably based on knowledge of the hypercomplex structure of the human brain. It would be impossible seriously to describe the brain, the organ of organic unification and of psychism, as just another organ.

What the biologist describes, then, is his scientific knowledge of the degree of complexity of different beings. Formerly it was useful to eliminate consciousness from the concerns of the specialist in the body, in order to escape the error of believing the biologist could know consciousness. That cannot be done today. Certainly the neurophysiologist does not want to replace the psychologist or the metaphysician by telling us what consciousness is or by studying its manifestations in their specific aspects of behavior or interiority. But he does establish the neurophysiology of consciousness, describing its cerebral conditions and linking up the degree of consciousness with the degree of brain. A rationalist and atheistic neurophysiologist, L. Lapique, can conclude that our reflective consciousness requires the cell to have a kind of rudimentary consciousness impossible to a robot. It is plainly not in the name of metaphysics (a reproach often made of Teilhard) but in the name of pure science that he comes to this conclusion.

The biologist sees that what is important for a being is its interior organization which measures its complexity. He consequently has the right to say that the passage from nonliving to living, though it is an advance as important as the advance to reflection, does not occur without leaving discernable analogies. Inanimate beings are not merely phenomena. They are beings at a less complex level of organization which have, therefore, a less complex interior unable to attain true psychism. Consequently, the Teilhardian perspective, far from being a debatable philosophy, is the purest science. In the evolutionary perspective of cosmogenesis where the inanimate is the preparation or *pre-life* of the animate, it does not restrict itself to descriptions of beings, but also situates them in a perspective of complexification wherein more complex beings descend from older, more simple ones.

Teilhard does not stop with such a description of the levels of organization and interiority. He further offers us an *energetic* description: to the classic energy of the physicist, he opposes a radial energy or energy of centricity which would be the measure of organization. On this point, some thought they had caught Teilhard right in the act of philosophizing. What is this mysterious energy? We know today that Teilhard was simply ahead of the scientific knowledge of his time and not philosophizing. The cybernetic theory of information shows us that what is important is not the gross energy of alimentation but the fractional *energy of information,* which has a far higher functional value and which we recognize as an energy because it is the reverse of entropy.

The task of proving with the aid of neurophysiology that the inwardness of things is a scientific reality is a very considerable one. But Teilhard goes further to show that, for him, this increased complexity is an *amorization.* A being that is more complex, more centered, more unified is not only richer in the static aspect of being, but also possesses an affective aspect, due to a more active centricity, of greater interaction among its components.

Here again, this view, foreign to scientists and looking like philosophy to philosophers, does not consist in assigning human love to our cells. It does mean refusing to neglect a fundamental aspect first of biology and finally of the entire cosmos. A superior being is this: not the juxtaposition of millions of cells, but the disappearance of their individuality which lends itself to the unity of the whole. Why, starting from a single cell, the egg, do we end up with a multicellular being, if not because an affinity, whose physiochemical basis is still little known, operates to maintain the groups of sister cells? These cells go on differentiating so successfully that each of them is of service to all and all are of service to each. Their solidarity is such that cell division is limited to preservation of the form of the whole. Only cells in a culture or cancerous cells, no longer obedient to this rule of solidarity, have a limitless capacity for division. Within an organism there is no room for cellular egocentricity because each cell is an element of the whole.

What is loving each other, but desiring each other's good? The organism unconsciously loves itself; that is, it has automatic regulators which allow it to fulfill the needs of the cells. The regulating nerve centers which are responsible for this, and which are seated at the base of the brain, are truly the active *center of unification* which gives the organism its higher individuality. At the level of this center are not only the physiological mechanisms which insure the constancy of the interior milieu, but also those instinctive behavior patterns which insure, for instance, correct nutrition. Automatically, without need for thought or choice, the animal is induced by its physiological state to seek the right amount of the right food. These responses have an unconscious affective coloring. That is, they are attracted by what is good, agreeable, and repelled by what is bad, repulsive, disagreeable. Even instinctive, unconscious conduct is not neutral but composed of attractions and repulsions.

Among less complex beings, these unconscious automatisms of love suffice to explain conduct, for their upper level of true consciousness is abridged. In man, on the other hand, this rudimentary level of consciousness gives place to the upper level of the brain, to reflective consciousness. In particular, if organic needs rising from the lower brain do persist, and we do become conscious of them, we no longer have the animal automatism necessary to proper fulfillment of our needs. We must find what we need by taking thought and choosing to act for the well-being of our organism. Within limits, set by our needs and by the dangers of excess, egotism is our duty, a duty to consider our health and to find pleasure in proper satisfaction of need. The joy of being alive, and of being in good health, is an essential dimension of our psychobiological organism. Thus, man's more complex cerebral organization substitutes a more conscious love for the unconscious love of the cells and the automatic protective mechanisms.

Reciprocally, and parallel to that aspect of inwardness which in the inanimate is analogous to consiousness, we may make a further observation. We see there is an undeniable consonance of the human love that is the chosen defense of our unified being, and the interattraction of cells, the cellular unification that imposes form and function adapted to varying diverse elements, and physiochemical attractions between atoms and molecules which have justly been named affinities. All this is expressed in certain elementary physiochemical properties, but may be studied scientifically as the physics of unification and integration. If evolution is complexification, it is because there is an elementary sympathy between elementary particles. One might well expect disorder and disorganization to be more prevalent in the world. Objectively they are not. Forces of attraction are at work to favor and defend increased complexity. Under scientific observation, as the subject of scientific inquiry before becoming the subject of philosophical reflection, these forces appear to be matter's most essential property.

The science of love deals not only with attractions

that underlie the maintenance of superior individuals, and the possible fusion of elementary individuals into a higher individuality runs across the question of attraction between individuals. We need more than nourishment alone. Living beings need beings like themselves. This is true for sexuality and, in more general fashion, is true for all the socialized species, among which individuals cannot find equilibrium alone, and *need others*. Animal sexual need is an automatic reaction provoked by the very centers of the brain which are adjacent to those producing hunger reactions. Under the stimulus of sexual hormones, there arise both sexual appetite, which accompanies genital activation and is only secondarily conscious, and sexual behavior, which induces the animal to perform as required to assure its sexuality, without having to learn how. Among inferior creatures, the butterfly for example, sexuality is a pure automatic reflex set off in the male by an odor the female emits. There is no knowledge of another through individual choice. On the other hand, the brains of birds and mammals have progressed to a point at which, before the automatic reflexes of coupling occur, choice and courtship take place, indicating the emergence of love in the true sense.

Thus it becomes apparent how reaffirmation of the evolutionary perspective that is in a true sense naturalistic, disproves the old false relativism that ignored the *levels of different beings*. Far from opposing morality, this confirms it by showing mankind the spiritual level of mastered love corresponding to our level of cerebration. Man's principal sexual organ is his superior brain that is responsible both for the superior aspects of his love and the possibility of mastering his genital reflexes, a possibility we use poorly because we know little about it. Here we find, really, the essential difference of the human level of amorization: automatic sexual need persists but the means of satisfying it are learned rather than instinctive. Ideally, it is a humanized love respectful of persons; practically, due to the absence of knowledge, it is an automatic preconception. It is natural for animals to be guided by instinct; if man thinks he is obeying instincts which he does not have, he dehumanizes himself, imitating animals rather than being guided by his superior nature with its reflective understanding.

Thus, the psychology of sexual love reestablishes unity between spiritual and carnal love. Purely carnal love denatures man; permanent monogamous marriage, based on love and including self-mastery, is the only natural carnal union for the human species.

In regard to the social order, we view our relation to it as a matter of taste or a duty; we often think of socialization with dread as an attack on our individuality. One of the errors most commonly and most unjustly ascribed to Teilhard is that he emphasizes the social at the expense of the individual. That is because we commonly and unjustly ignore the full significance of the actual fact of our social nature, which we prefer to see only in its cultural, superior, human aspect. Man, however, is a social species and in every social being a new level of amorization appears: a need for others so real that the individual alone cannot find his equilibrium and may even sometimes find life impossible. This affective and instinctive automatic response, which is the need for others, rises from centers at the base of the brain and marks every social being in its flesh. Among animals the need is met by social instincts which regulate a common life. Among men, there is no longer a true social instinct; the need is dismissed in favor of egoistic expansion of the individual personality. It takes examples like those of the dehumanized wolf-children or the disorders of hospitalized men to make us understand that there is no normal man outside of normal human relationships.

It is not necessary for us either to search for or to fear socialization; we need simply become aware that it is part of our nature. In ages past, the average uncultured man had a personality that scarcely emerged from the collective mass. Thanks to cultural and psychological progress, which is a social process, personality has progressed until we may forget its social dimension and think we can do without or even oppress others. But the fact is that man is neither normal nor natural outside of a natural society, that is, one which establishes a just balance between the needs of others and the needs of individual expansion, the love of self and the love of others. What was an automatic response in the animal becomes in mankind the *duty to love*. Yet the social reality is not like the biological process which brought about the disappearance of individual cellularity. It is different because society is not an entity in itself; rather it is the interrelations of individuals who relinquish none of their liberty except in order to safeguard the liberty of others.

Plainly, insisting with Teilhard on the importance of this degree of amorization does not lead to substituting biology for sociology; instead, it enables the sociologist to take into account society's organic infrastructures, which are all the more important in that they play a large role in human society where they are widely misunderstood. In comparing insect societies where all is automatic and on an elementary biological level with vertebrate societies where cultural and conscious factors dominate, one must give objective recognition to how different levels of social amorization relate to different levels of organic complexity.

Man, do as he may, can never evade the consequences of his superior nature; it obliges him on pain of disequilibrium to situate himself at the higher level of conscious love. Relativist thinking in sociology might suggest that it is possible to accept social inequalities and injustice and yet remain balanced. But it is not in any way possible. Bio-sociological conditions are such that a slave held below livable minimum satisfaction of his needs, especially his spiritual needs, will be unbalanced; and so will the tyrant who puts himself above the human condition in making himself all-powerful. Obedience to the laws of amorization is the basis of social and political wisdom as well as the body's unconscious wisdom.

III

Future of Amorization:
Prospects in Agapology

"We are anxious and disquieted when we recognize that modern attempts at human collectivization end up, contrary both to theoretical preconceptions and to our expectations, only in the lowering and enslavement of consciousness. . . . Love alone, for the good reason that it alone takes hold of the radical inwardness of beings and there joins them together, is capable—and this is a fact of daily experience—of completing the beings as beings, by making them unite. At what moment is it that two lovers really reach the most complete self-possession, if not that in which they say they are lost in each other? In truth, love continually effects the magical gesture, the gesture (deemed contradictory) which personalizes as it totalizes, in the couple, in the team, round about us. And why may it not repeat, one day, on a global scale, what it thus accomplishes daily in smaller dimensions? Humanity; the spirit of the earth; synthesis of individuals and of peoples; the paradoxical conciliation of the element and the whole, of unity and multiplicity: for the world to embody these things deemed utopian, yet biologically necessary, is it not enough to imagine our ability to love developed until it embraces the whole of mankind and of the earth? A universal love: not only is it psychologically possible, it is, further, the only complete and final way in which we are able to love."

When the paleontologist Teilhard tells us the meaning of evolution, we accept it. But we find it scandalous and contrary to true science if he quits his fossils to foretell the future, assuring us that otherwise the past does not interest him. In the name of science, Western historians and sociologists have already rejected Marxist theory of historical meaning, based on examination of human history. What can be said if this thesis is defended in the name of biology? It would be called naturalism, inadmissibly forgetful of the fact that human history is of an order entirely different from animal history. Teilhard knew that difference well. It was he who pointed out the revolution of the step up to reflective thought and of the advance to liberty, responsibility and cultural progress from generation to generation which is due to the human brain and which gives human societies a dimension different in kind from any found in animal societies. Yet it was also he who showed paleontologists smothered in details that evolution has a meaning.

So, having given full stature to the phenomenon of man, that is, to the scientific side of the human being, in the same way he has a perfect right to show historians and sociologists lost in history's incoherent vicissitudes that there exists a measuring rod for the human value of a civilization. That measuring rod is: to what degree is it favorable to human nature's fullest flowering? Man is man from the outset, that is, in the higher degree of love. But he differs from the animal which obeys its instincts with small need to learn and reflect, and indeed with no ability to do

so. Man is true to his aptitudes and nature only insofar as he learns to understand them and fulfill
them properly. There is a kind of technical education which focuses on minimizing the essential values
of man's heart. This school opposes and juxtaposes
reason and feeling as being higher and lower and
quite forgets that in man heartfelt love is not ir-
rational, inferior, elementary affectivity. Thanks to
the prefrontal lobes of the human brain, human love
is the union, on a higher level, of the rational and the
affective which gives reflective thought its full dimension in the order of love.

Starting from biology, Teilhard simultaneously opposes both those who deny all meaning to history
and those Marxists who recognize a meaning but tend
to turn it into the automatic destroyer of individual
freedom, which can require hate as a duty in class
warfare. He shows us a future in which the whole
earth is covered by the ideal society which he calls
the *noosphere*. Use of this word might imply a cultural union. But in reality, what makes the noosphere
the ideal human society is that it is a personalist
society where social relations are based on love. It
is an *agaposphere*.

Too utopian, some might say, and whatever we see
points in the opposite direction. The point is that the
noosphere, just like whatever else is natural to mankind, will not be realized without great effort. The
noosphere, which is within the meaningful continuity
of evolution and of history, is the summit of amorizing socialization, that good socialization which John
XXIII in *Mater et Magistra* recently recommended to
our efforts. We shall not escape socialization because man is socialized by nature. But if we are not
careful, our socialization may take the form either of
anarchic liberalism in which man is desocialized within the crowd or of tyrannical totalitarianism which is

equally fatal to the building of a healthy and balanced society. Alone, man is not able to save himself or find his equilibrium. He is by nature interdependent and finds equilibrium only in interdependence. Amorization continues but it is no longer an irresistible automatic process. It is given into our hands, which are responsible for completing the construction of earth. To show the utopia of the noosphere is therefore simply to offer a real goal to the specialists who survey the society of tomorrow.

Teilhard removes us from the absurd and shows us that life is meaningful; he asks that we abandon sterile discord in favor of working out the common front of human advancement. To think that he is therefore an optimist and ignorant of evil is to misunderstand completely. It is for the very reason that love, while natural to man, is much more difficult than indifference or unnatural hate that Teilhard insists so much upon it. How easy it would be to let go, to be discouraged and say that no one can do anything about it, that evil will triumph for a time here below. But such reasoning is an act against love; it means being less than a man and a normal individual; it is to be immature and, as regards the meaning of history, uncivilized; it is to injure oneself while injuring others. Hate does exist and we must struggle against it. But however strong and active it may be, hate is nothing other than the counterpart of love, the pathology of love. Though the human level is of another order, once again Teilhard has analogies to show us. In a world which is imperfect in that it is not God and is merely on the way to improvement, the ability to rise also necessarily implies the ability to fall.

IV
Metaphysics and
Mysticism of Love

Thus, moving in the direction of Teilhard's thrust, we have all the elements that constitute a real science of love. One day we might even see this science developing autonomously and becoming a new scientism; materialists might then declare that though the spiritual-minded were right to insist on the importance of love, love is a simple objective fact with no metaphysical implications.

There is something tragic in comparing the common sense of a Marseilles docker who is converted by seeing the beauty of living things, with the reaction of a scientist versed in nuclear acids or biological evolution who finds therein not further reasons for belief but an insuperable obstacle to faith. So the great strength of Teilhard is not simply in making scientists abandon a purblind positivist scientism in favor of going on fearlessly to the very limit of the possibilities of science. It is, even more, that he stands witness to the fact that *science is not enough*. There is no separation between the phenomenon of man and the divine milieu. He makes it evident that the "scientific formula" opens out widely into metaphysics, if only at the Omega point. It is fairly easy to distinguish what is purely scientific; we need only compare "the phenomenon of man" with the "evolution in action" of Julian Huxley, Teilhard's friend who is not a believer. There are also unpublished writings in which Teilhard indicates even more plainly the need for unity of science, metaphysics, and mysticism in his total view.

Teilhard is not technically a philosopher, yet when dissatisfied with scientists' positions he offered them a frame of reference for a scientific concept of the earth and of mankind. In a like manner he speaks to philosophers. He addresses himself to those lost in their divisiveness, split between the camp of traditional metaphysicans shut up in concepts inadequately related to science's new "universe in cosmogenesis", and the camp of modern philosophers who are as relativist as the scientists and who are shut up in a spiritual phenomenology which denies the metaphysics of natures and essences. Teilhard is very conscious that the development of the scientific (and seemingly materialistic) explanation calls for a metaphysics of matter and creation, and he reminds us that Thomism has contributed some elements for one, whence his interest in the work of Father Sertillanges. What analogy could be closer to complexification and the inwardness of things than that of substantial form, vegetative soul, animal soul and human soul? For all its spiritual nature, the substantial form of the human soul unites with matter to give it its meaning, as the form of a body which would not exist without it; so, the scientist's cerebral superiority becomes the metaphysician's superiority of soul.

Teilhard goes still further. To give an account of this world in a state of amorizing complexification, Teilhard proposes a dynamic metaphysics that is a *metaphysics of union*, for which he sketches the main features. "In classical metaphysics, it has been customary to deduce the world from the idea of being, considered as irreducibly primitive. . . . I shall try to show here that a dialectic more supple and rich than others becomes possible if one supposes at the start that a being, far from representing an ultimate and singular idea, is in reality definable (genetically at least, if not ontologically) by a particular movement indissolubly associated with it, that of union. It follows that one can write, depending on the case: to be = to be uniting oneself or to be uniting others (active form); to be = to be united and unified by another (passive form)."

He can in this way develop a whole metaphysics of the creation by the God of love. Some have called Teilhard a pantheist. It is assuredly easy to find numerous passages in which he addresses his love to matter and to the universe but, behind appearances, it was always true divine reality that he saw. "And there it was, at the center of the turbulence, a growing whorl of light that had the softness and mobility of a glance. . . . A warmth spread abroad, that was no longer the hard radiation of a single source but a rich emanation of living flesh. . . . The blind and wild immensity grew expressive, personal. Its formless layers flowed, following the features of an ineffable countenance. A Being sketched itself everywhere, attractive as a soul, palpable as a body, vast as the skies, a Being mingled with things while yet distinct from them, superior to their substance with which it was draped and yet taking shape in them. . . ."

It is in the name of the very arguments of materialistic evolution that Teilhard discloses to us not the rationalized God of philosophers, a concept, but the transcendent personal God of love in Christ. Science seems to say that matter, by its own powers alone, arrives at man, a personal, loving being. Is it not most unreasonable to assign matter such capacities? If it does have them, then it must be the Christian God—or, more accurately, then it must be the Creator, the organizer and inventor of love who makes himself manifest behind it. The secret Mover must be more love than the end product of evolutionary movement, man, is.

What makes understanding hard for us is that in rejecting the pantheistic error which denies God by making him the non-existent world soul, we have fallen into another equally prejudicial heresy which Teilhard chooses to combat because it leads to denial of God in the name of science. Hunted out of the world, the idea of God does not take refuge elsewhere, in ineffectual transcendence. If he be super-structure, he is useless and does not exist. Yet pantheism, though wrong in denying God's transcendent reality, was right in affirming God's secret presence at the heart of reality, his immanence. Creation is not the doing of a human craftsman; it is the metaphysical dependence of all that is created. The laws of what is apparently scientific materialism are not really opposed to the true God; they logically require him. They are the laws of creation. He who believes in the God of love finds love in the world and he who has found love in the world has scientific confirmation that God is love.

To love one's neighbor as oneself is not enough for human nature. God is not the most distant, but the most near. Man needs an ideal; the most human ideal is a personal ideal with which a personal relationship is possible. The superior level of man's amorization is the prayer relationship to the God of love.

The biological evolution continuing through history, having as norm and meaning a rise which is more union, more coherence, more convergence, necessarily demands a source of attraction which is more love. This source of attraction, which is above and ahead, has the power of amorization only if it is real, if it be not merely a false god who comes but the true God outside of time who has been, is and shall be, world without end. In amorizing the world, in amorizing society, man is on the march toward the God of love, that Omega point of supreme convergence, a view which Teilhard proposes to us in harmony with Christian eschatology.

Teilhard's noosphere might be envisaged only in its aspect of a sociological norm required of us if we wish to survive and to live fully; and, in that case, one might imagine a purely natural ultimate point of convergence. That is the position of Julian Huxley. Teilhard's logic, in line with his faith, could not possibly stop there. If there were only the natural, if that rise of love were to terminate finally in the total death of the individual and of the species, it would be absurd and there would be no motivation in it for the efforts of mankind. But it is precisely because cosmogenesis does have a meaning that it has a complete one.

The individual should grow in love all his life. To be faithful to the dynamism of the rise of human nature, he should become more himself, avoiding the risk of failure through ceaseless effort. In growing, the individual makes others grow and enlarges mankind's possibilities. This progressive maturation in love is a good use of the body, which is increasingly spiritualized thereby. It could not possibly end up in nothingness; rather, it occasions the meeting with the source of all rising, the encounter in passing to another level of being with the God of love. The view of the natural norm agrees with the traditional thesis. Man does not make himself—which is to say, save himself—alone, but through love in his heart which admits God's grace there, though prejudice prevents him from reaching knowledge of the true God.

As we have seen, Teilhard's view of the future includes no absolute guarantee of success. Success does lie within the norm of the world and the will of God, certainly. Success is natural and failure is against nature. But everything depends on liberty and human effort. However, this view is also not that of pelagian naturalism which asserts that at the end of time God's kingdom will come on earth as a result of man's work. It is man's duty to grow until he dies; he then passes into another order of being entirely.

Only superficially could Teilhard's view seem contrary to the destructive visions of the Apocalypse. For nature to confront divine love which is fire must always mean a conflagration, a change of state. Teilhard in *The Divine Milieu* definitely insisted on our difficulty in accepting those natural diminutions, like those of old age or the expectation of death, which are necessary for us to attain our definitive dimensions. The glorification of the individual like that of the world is prepared through natural amorization, but its final achievement is first of all supernatural. To the degree that the nature which is confronted by fire is fully love, it is in the happiness of heaven; on the other hand, that which is hate cannot meet with God save in destructive suffering. There will always be an apocalyptic overthrow but its consequence will depend on what we have made of the earth and mankind.

The God of love, by his immanence the secret of love for the world and man in construction, yet remains distant from us because of our weakness which makes us follow the unnatural, easy road of downfall more readily than we try the difficult though natural road of the upward rise. A being of flesh has natural

temptations to denature itself which would fix it at a
level below its nature and cut it off from God. There
is a profound truth here, perfectly expressed in that
dogma of original sin which always presented itself to
Teilhard as a certitude sometimes betrayed by an
excessively traditional, incomplete presentation. Original sin, which is a human responsibility that sepa-
rates us from God, comes from our insufficiency at
the start.

"After what I have just said on my conviction that
a personal, divine term to human evolution does
exist, it might seem that a serene and luminous future must open out before me in my life. Doubtless,
death must then seem to me just like one of those
sleeps after which we never question that we shall
see a splendid morning dawn. But it is not like that at
all. Certain, more and more certain, that I must walk
into existence as if, at the end of the universe, Christ
waits for me, yet I experience no particular assurance
of his existence. Believing is not seeing. I imagine
that I, as much as anyone, walk among the shadows
of faith. No, I am sure God does not conceal himself
just so that we may look for him, any more than he
lets us suffer to increase our merit. Quite the contrary; bending over the creation which rises toward
him, he works with all his might to beatify and illuminate it. Like a mother, he watches his new-born.
But our eyes do not yet know how to perceive him.
Will we not need precisely the whole length of the
ages for our vision to be open to the light? Our
doubts, like our ills, are the price and very condition
of a universal achievement. And under those conditions, I accept that I walk to the end on a road of
which I am more and more sure, toward horizons
more and more lost in fog."

In the short work of which the preceding quotation
is the conclusion (*Comment je crois*, Peking, 1934)

Teilhard, having stated his faith in the world, his faith in the spirit, in immortality, in personality, puts the various religions in one way or another to the test. How do they accord with the evolutionary concept of a world in the state of amorization? He concludes objectively that no solution can be found in the partial truths glimpsed in Oriental religions of pantheistic tendencies which submerge the person in the great All. Nor does the answer lie in the "religions" of forward-march, the scientific materialisms which in denying God to protect the person make the person absurd and incomplete. What is needed lies between them; the personalizing God, which is the Christian concept, is the one solution. But Teilhard shows us that in practice Christianity is often so poorly understood that it becomes a disincarnate religion in which only personal salvation counts.

True Christianity, however, gives matter and history their fullest meaning. God was made flesh—there it is, all of it! He gave human history its fullest meaning. Some have tried to separate sacred history from profane; on the contrary, what is needed is, without confusing them, to understand what sacred history really is: that of personal dealings between God and man, that of God's love for man, which gives human history its meaning.

Man, freely charged with completing the work of amorization, yet understanding it little, needed a nearer God, more closely tied to human history. For Teilhard, the true meaning of evolution and of history, God's creative love, is to arrive finally at a human love capable of being united in Christ to the divine nature. In the incarnation, love is stronger than in creation. But, given the full freedom of God respecting the full freedom of mankind, his creatures, the incarnation could not logically, in this imperfect world, culminate elsewhere than upon the cross. God brought himself closer and we did not want him to rule over us. Kill him! We reject him and that rejection only unleashes a love still greater, which ties him still closer to us. "There is no greater love than to give one's life."

Once more Teilhard here—as for natural history and for history—only suggests his view's main lines to indicate the accord between traditional theology, which he does not develop, and the natural perspective. The incarnation and the cross, important as they are, are only a beginning. We cannot consider the Man-Christ and forget the Word; we cannot think of the Man-God as an accident of history. On the contrary he is the setting in motion of true history, the end of prehistory. What is the construction of the noosphere but the building of the mystical body of Christ? History becomes *Christogenesis*. Society implies a leader but every human leader risks becoming an oppressor. Teilhard does not envision at all that persons should vanish into our society as cells do within an organism. However, the comparison with a body retains a value. Here the unifying factor, the head, must, in order to avoid depersonalizing the constitutive elements, be hyperpersonal and thus on another plane; and yet there is no other natural plane. It is Christ, as the universal Christ. That salvation which he came to give us is precisely this bringing us together in unity.

"Catholicism," Teilhard tells us, "had at first glance disappointed me by its narrow opinions of the world and by its lack of understanding of the role of matter." He was referring to the ways faith is frequently formularized, which are in fact contrary to revelation. "It was then that the universal Christ appeared to me." "The world about me grows divine; and yet neither do these flames destroy me nor do these floods dissolve me. For, unlike the false monisms which move through passivity toward unconsciousness, the 'pan-Christianism' that I discover situates union as the ultimate term of a laborious differentiation. I shall become the other only in becoming absolutely myself. I shall come to the spirit only in freeing to their limit the powers of matter. The total Christ is consummate and reachable only at the ultimate term of universal evolution. In him I have found what my being dreamed of: a personalized universe whose domination personalizes me. . . . Some have reproached me with being an innovator. In truth, the more I have meditated on the magnificent cosmic attributes St. Paul unstintingly applies to Christ, the more I have been aware that Christianity takes on its full value only when carried to universal dimensions."

And in his last work, *Le Christique,* he adds, "In truth, from the instant when, instead of isolating it and opposing it to what is moving, it is resolutely 'wired in' to the world in motion. Christianity, exhausted though it may seem to the eyes of our contemporary gentiles, instantly and integrally again picks up its initial power of attraction and charm. Because then, as a result of being 'switched into gear', it alone among all the forms of adoration born in the course of human history manifests the astonishing capacity to totally energize, by amorizing, both the powers of growth and life and the powers of diminution and death at the heart and on the way of the noogenesis wherein we find ourselves engaged."

It is animated with this faith in the world which is impossible to dissociate from his faith in Christ that the priest-scientist Teilhard went up to the altar of his Mass to offer and to consecrate the world, an indispensable function of amorization where the Christ in the eucharist takes the relationship with matter that enables him through our bodies to become the instrument of the higher amorization of our beings. "Because . . . you, my God, have given me an irresistible sympathy for everything that stirs indistinct in matter—because I recognize, irremediably, in myself much more than a child of heaven, a son of earth—I shall go up in thought, this morning, upon the high places, charged with the hopes and anguish of my mother; and there—strong with a priesthood you alone, I believe, have given me—on all that in human flesh readies itself to be born or to die under the sun then rising, I shall call down the Fire . . . Christ glorious, Influence secretly diffused deep within matter and Center blindingly radiant where the unnumbered fibres of the multiple come together; Power implacable as the world and warm as life; you whose brow is snow, whose eyes are fire, whose feet are more gleaming than molten gold, you whose hands imprison the stars; you who are the first and the last, the living, the dead and the resurrected, you who bring together in your superabundant unity every charm, every taste, every strength, every estate; it is you whom my being called with a desire vast as the universe: truly you are my Lord and my God!"

So the secret of the world is love and we have only to choose whether to love each other or to perish. But we do not know what love is. One may love (or adore) anything. One may love candy, interior decoration, a dog, a wife, a friend, the poor, humanity, an ideal, God. What can there be in common among all these loves? Shall we find the answer in Freud? Is it *libido*, Eros, which is at the heart of being, with all pleasurable affectivity understood as sexual? Though there is some truth in it, we are well aware that if it be the whole answer, it diminishes love. Teilhard, prophet of a newer age, confirms Freud in placing love at the heart of being; but love is single and the truth of carnal love is that it is quickened through spiritual love. Poor fragments of love, adrift in a mad world that does not know how to love! There is but one duty, to learn how to love. There is but one happiness, to know how to love. He knew it well, that solitary who saw but could not make visible, who felt the value of the great secret of unity which God had confided to him but who could not disseminate it as a unified whole: not either the world or God, but the world through him and in him and with him!

One day in Peking he did formulate the secret of happiness which is man's common hope. His message, published at last, can now reach all men: "Pessimism and return to the past; enjoyment of the present moment; leap toward the future: the tired; the sensual; the eager—three basic attitudes toward life. As a consequence, three inevitably opposed forms of happiness: happiness of tranquillity, happiness of pleasure, happiness of growth and development." And Teilhard goes on to show the choice of the true way: "Let the tired pessimists slip behind. Let the sensual stretch out in bourgeois comfort on the slope. And let us join without hesitation the group of those who want to risk the climb to the ultimate summit."

What does life ask of us? "No longer simply to develop oneself, nor even simply to give oneself to another who is one's equal; but further, to submit one's life and bring it to one greater than oneself. In other words, first be, then love, and at last adore. Such are the natural phases of our personalization: happiness of growing, happiness of loving, happiness of adoration."

PART TWO
Teilhard de Chardin
and the
Optimism of the Cross

Not indefinite progress—a hypothesis contradicted by the convergent nature of noogenesis—but an ecstasy, beyond the dimensions and borders of the visible universe.

Ecstasy in concord or in discord; but in either case, due to an inner excess of tension.

The only biological issue suitable and conceivable for the phenomenon of man.

THE PHENOMENON OF MAN

V
What Are We To Do?
What Can We Think?

"A ridiculous atom, lost in an inert and immeasurable cosmos, he knows that his feverish activity is but a tiny, ephemeral, local phenomenon, without meaning and without aim. . . . Fending off the fruitless vertigo of the infinite, deaf to the frightening silence of space, he will force himself to become noncosmic just as the universe is non-human; fiercely turned in upon himself, he will dedicate himself humbly and earthily to the achievement of his poor intentions, which he will pretend to treat with the same seriousness as he would show if they were directed to eternal goals."

Does this disillusioned statement of Jean Rostand's really contain the scientific secret of the world? Shall we, under such conditions, have enough moral courage and stoicism to go on living while trying to ignore it?

We can ignore it by taking refuge in pleasure: either that of careless and selfish laziness, or that of hunting down brief temporal satisfactions following the whim of the moment, or that of the absurd but earnestly engaged verbalism of the existentialists (yet a moment does come when words no longer solace the horror of objects).

However, acts become more serious by becoming fraternal, in the union of everyone in order to humanize a hostile world: the proposal of Camus; the Marxist invitation to roll up our sleeves and further a partial sense of man's ephemeral history which will assure us of "tomorrows that sing" along with, perhaps, scientific immortality—that opium—in a conquered cosmos.

Among these diverse options, look for some one adventure big enough for man's ardent heart, communicable enough so that young people be not led to the frightful solidarity of useless violence where they dissipate themselves by destroying their aimless energies in desperate leather-jacketed bands—being less hypocritical and submissive than their elders who perform strictly within legal limits, while the poor go on dying in hunger, misery and solitude.

Yet is the worst entirely certain? "Say, if it were true," they sing. If what were true? What took place once, in a canton of the Roman empire. That Jesus, at the wedding in Cana—didn't he die on a cross? Following Peter, Christians tell us that he rose again from the dead, and that that changes everything.

Obviously, that does open out to us a heaven totally unlike the heaven of the cosmonauts. Yet, in his time, the Athenian intellectuals didn't follow Paul; what can you expect from today's scientific atheism?

Why expect, anyway? So you can live exiled in the hell of this valley of tears and suffer as much as you can to make sure of your salvation, turning down all the joys of this world so you can fly from sin. You think that's an attractive idea?

"Let us admit it. If the neo-humanisms of the

... diminish our humanity under too ... surviving forms of theism (starting ...anity) for their part tend to under-hu- ... in the rarified atmosphere of a sky too ...il systematically closed off from the vast ...zons and the great winds of cosmogenesis, they no longer really sense with the earth—an earth whose internal friction they can still soften, like a soothing oil, but whose sources of action they cannot (as they should) animate." Who said that? The Reverend Father Teilhard de Chardin in his last piece of writing, *Le Christique.* Then does he agree that Christianity is no solution?

Don't jump to conclusions. Hear what follows. "And at this point the strength of the *Christique* bursts forth, as it has appeared to us here below, born of the progressive encounter within our understanding, between the cosmic exigencies of the incarnate Word and the spiritual potential of a convergent universe. At the heart of the divine milieu a disciplined composition is coming into being, as we have seen, between the forces of heaven and the forces of earth. An exact conjunction results between the ancient God of above-and-beyond and the new God of up-ahead."

A new religion? No wonder Rome has been cautious! No, it is not that at all. Rather it is just a question of shedding light on the encounter between the theological demands of a science that is better understood and more complete, and Christian revelation in its full earthly and human sense. That is what has been done by those who have known how to read Teilhard (which not everyone has been able to do): Wildiers, de Lubac, Smulders, Rabut . . .

But we are not about to plunge here and now into a full-scale examination of all theology and all science. We know Teilhard is the "witness for love" in proving the identity of the love at the heart of the

world with the divine love. We know how that optimist tells us the sense of history in a world that is
not absurd will lead us forward, toward a marvelous
society where each person will flourish, where God
will come to dwell. Can we survive on that dream, we
who are in the yesterday of that tomorrow, in the
cold, the mud, the blood? "How pleasant it is to
sleep on the maternal breast of the globe, instead of
waking up upon a cross" is what Charbonneau said
in arguing that Teilhard is the "prophet of a totalitarian age".

He did put his finger on the essential problem. Is
the "new-born" Christianity of Teilhard like that of
John XXIII or is it a Christianity without the cross?

The priest-mystic Teilhard lived in union with his
master who was crucified (and gloriously resurrected,
let us remember). Not a theologian, it was not for
him to scrutinize the mystery of the cross, nor was it
his task to speak of it. Yet what we want to show
briefly and sketchily is that, contrary to statements
frequently made, the entire work of Teilhard lies
within the shadow (the light) of the cross. His every
thought as a scientist turns toward its mystery, which
he incites us to look for within the Church in the hope
of better understanding it. From his viewpoint as a
"son of the earth" the redemptive cross which gra-
ciously amorizes the world seems in some sense as if
evoked by the needs of matter and of technique.

Why is this? Because he who was incontestably a
professor of happiness and a master of the joy of
living, he who stirred us to see the positive, the good,
everywhere, was nevertheless a lucid realist who saw
and shared lovingly in the suffering of men (in spite
of what his blind enemies wrongly claim). We may
say with Madeleine Madaule that his optimism is
dramatic—that is, a combat costing blood and tears—
but not tragic, never despairing. Anguish, yes—but

anguish in the effort to succeed and to not fail in the work which God gives us and for which he gives us his grace.

Yet Teilhard is not the only one reproached for an optimism which is truly Christian hope, the "little-girl hope" of Péguy. Good Pope John declared, "They say the pope is too optimistic, that he sees only what is good. But I do not know how to separate myself from the Lord who did nothing other than spread good abroad and who emphasized Yes more than No. . . . There is bad, there are weaknesses and a turmoil of powerful temptations in the modern world, but the good is there too."

Teilhard the seer offered the wretched world fire, that is, the love-shattered heart of the Savior on the cross. "It isn't truly enough that I die while receiving communion," he wrote. "Teach me to receive communion while dying." A crucifying communion completed a crucified life in the encounter: Easter Day, 1955.

VI
The Rise and
the Universal Dread

If Teilhard is useful to men today, to the contemporaries of atomic bombs, concentration camps and scientific torture, it is because he shares their suffering. The Marxist cannot help but question himself, faced by Stalinism; the Liberal must face the September massacres; the Catholic, the Inquisition. We were appalled by Oradour—that crime of "good" soldiers obeying orders—but now there are countless Oradours; Dresden matches Hiroshima in horror (a duty, for the victory of the good?). So it is starting from the present that he has to demonstrate the possibility of good.

Hear what he says: "At every second, through all the cracks, the huge horrible thing breaks in—that which we force ourselves to forget is always there, separated from us by a simple partition: fire, plague, tempest, earthquake, the unleashing of obscure forces of behavior in an instant heedlessly carrying away what we have painfully put together and embellished with all our intelligence and our heart. So that I may not succumb to the temptation of reviling the universe and him who made it, make me adore it because

I see you hidden in it. The great word, Lord—repeat to me the word that at once reveals and operates: 'This is my body.' Truly, the Thing, vast and dark, the phantom, the tempest, if we like, is you. May we just believe. May we believe the harder and the more despairingly as reality seems the more threatening and irreducible. And then little by little we shall see the universal Horror relax and smile at us and enfold us in more-than-human arms. Because we shall have believed intensely on the earth, the earth will open before us the arms of God."

Evil in the world, the obvious scandal in apologetics for the God of love, is not first human evil. There are our inadequacies and sins, not those of monsters and gangsters but our own; we know well what we are capable of. The brutes of the concentration camps were not freaks. They might have been good fellows, good husbands, good fathers. Like us they might or might not have chosen to act for the good. If things go ill in our world of men, let us accuse ourselves.

However, we did not invent the microbe or the virus, nor are radioactivity and thalidomide the only causes of abnormal births; furthermore, all those who die in earthquakes are not victims of some architect's imprudence. This wondrous planet of men and living things is a dangerous milieu.

It is a fact of which Teilhard was well aware. There is little need to remind a biologist or a paleontologist that life is carnage, and that not accidentally but by its very nature. The herbivorous beast that eats the grass is meant to be eaten by carnivores and the flea is meant to bite us. Biological evolution is an incoherent luxuriance of life burgeoning in every direction and the unsuccessful attempts are fiercely eliminated in the struggle for existence. There is incoherence manifested in the suture lines of certain Mezozoic cephalopods, incoherence in those

giant reptiles abruptly extinct, absurdity in the ortho-
genetic progress toward a better form of life which
terminated in the death of a carnivore with canine
teeth that prevented it from eating. Is not all this
absurd, an absurdity that finally, accidentally, produces that absurd creature, man?

True enough, Teilhard would say, that is, if you
forget the most important part: that through it all,
something great is being produced in the rising of
biological organization and of brain which makes possible more consciousness, more freedom, more love.

For man to exist, for saints to live their lives, for the
woman Mary to have said *Fiat*, for God to take
human nature, for society in its growth to give Christ
his mystical body, for the matter that will be glorified at the end of time to be more beautiful—for the
sake of all this, may we not suppose it necessary to
accept the sacrifice of grass and herbivore, the risk
of degenerative power in virus or parasite, the rejection of the over-adapted from the path of progress?

For they in their vague consciousness suffered for
us, for Christ; just as, in Péguy's words, the Roman
legions unknowingly marched in his behalf. Interdependent with all life, we should love our inferior
brothers, first of all by being true men in that human
dignity they have painfully afforded us. Let us be
faithful to that rise of life provided by God's chosen
creatures, the first fish to leave the sea and live,
the first primate standing on two legs and looking
up at the sky.

But could it not have been accomplished without
so much suffering? The earth, which is not God, is
necessarily imperfect, the theologian says. But imperfect to such an extent? There are not only beings
wonderfully imperfect, harmonious in their downfall,
but beings cut short and diminished in value.

Teilhard tells us that these are the conditions of the rise. This evil would only be scandalous in a static cosmos conceived of as emerging complete, directly from God's hands. Once the Creator relies on his creation—that is, on the properties of matter—that creation recognizes it has a degree of autonomy, one which develops on the human level into our liberty which would not otherwise exist. Only a permanent, perpetual miracle of God, which is not the normal mode of creation, could keep the path of the rise open while preventing nuclear acids from undergoing degeneration.

Such evil is inseparable from cosmogenesis, of which it is the darker, reverse side. It might be thought of in the terms of thermodynamics: steam engines break down energy, expending one part of it in heat, and thereby produce power. Life does something similar: organization is produced through the negentropic breakdown of energy causing an increase in confusion as well as a rise in entropy.

A world in cosmogenesis is a world working and fighting to rise, progress, ripen; it is laboring to give birth and suffering to grow. This new aspect of the *disorders due to maturation* is what Teilhard suggests. It is a question of rising from multiplicity to unity. "God, to create, can proceed in only one way: [things being what they are in our universe, impossible to consider as otherwise] [1] arranging and unifying little by little, under his attractive influence, by using the tentative play of vast numbers, an immense multitude of elements at first infinitely numerous, extremely simple and scarcely conscious—then gradually fewer, more complex, and finally endowed with reflection. Now what is the inevitable counterpart of any success obtained through a process of this kind, if not the expenditure of a certain percent

[1] The parenthetical note is the author's.

as waste? Disharmonies or physical decomposition among preliving things, suffering among the living, sin in the area of freedom: no order taking shape that does not, at every step, imply disorder. In this ontological (or rather ontogenetic) condition of whatever participates there is nothing to lessen or limit the all-powerfulness of the Creator. Nor is there anything in any way tainted by Manicheanism. Pure, unorganized multiplicity is not in itself bad, but because it is multiple, that is, with its ordering essentially subject to the play of chance, it absolutely cannot progress toward unity without here and there engendering disorder—by statistical necessity. . . . Disorder is an inevitable by-product; it seems like a hardship inseparable from creation, like its shadow."

There is the law of nature. It is far from merry. Indeed, it calls forth the cross.

VII
A World Made Absurd

Man appears: there is the step up to reflection. Freedom? The perspectives all change and yet, in the drama of *analogy*, everything stays the same, or in other words, becomes more acute. Disorder becomes sin, bringing into play our responsibility to ourselves, others and God.

But can we move so crudely from irresponsible prehuman disorders to man's sin? We are aware that, without making excuses of them, there are factors that lessen our responsibility. There is, then, a level of human disorder that is not sin. It is harmful nonetheless. Ignorance, weakness, neglect, imprudence, prejudice—more than wrong, deliberately chosen, these are the causes of what goes ill in the world of man, and that, among normal individuals. Beyond that, there are all the anomalies, all the vast crowds of pathological motivations that drag down or destroy our freedom—this or that violent and dangerous man may be one who is brain-damaged, hyperthyroid or a neurotic symbolically expressing repressions, and would be better examined by a doctor than by a judge or a moral theologian. It is God alone who can judge a Hitler; but we may ask to what extent he was a madman incapable of responsible action, and how

57

far was Nietzsche restricted by the general paralysis, and again, to what extent did Nazis hypnotized by the liturgies of Nuremberg retain lucidity, especially the young ones brought up in that atmosphere. We may ask if we know what we might be capable of under mass hypnotism, under the spell of imitative behavior.

Teilhard has been accused of trying to minimize evil by making it statistical. But he does not tell us to confuse prehuman disorder and human disorder. He show us simply that evil in man is a consequence of the material origin of our makeup, though become much more serious.[2]

That is primarily because man, no longer having sound animal instincts, must learn how to behave like a man, how to do well, in order to be free. For man ignorance can become the source of monstrous deformation. In the second place, it is because man retains, even when no longer ignorant, the power to choose between good and evil.

That is the great drama of humanity: man's task is to finish creation by completing and bettering it, by causing order to increase. That is the human vocation, the dignity of a *co-creator* to which God calls man. In so doing, he himself should make progress. Instead, either voluntarily or involuntarily he fosters the growth of disorder. We live not in an absurd world but a world made absurd by human stupidity and sin.

History is therefore an inextricable tangle of good and evil. The juxtaposition and succession of civilizations and social structures seem to be a proliferation, on another plane, just as incoherent as that of species

---

[2] This makes him lenient so that he does not judge anyone as purely good or evil in doctrinaire fashion. He views with objective justice the intuitions and errors of Communism, present Democracy and Fascism. Some therefore call him Fascist or Communist, which is ridiculous.

in the course of evolution. Here Teilhard's contribution is to indicate, from his knowledge of evolution, that in spite of everything the progress of consciousness continues, becoming more generalized. Man does learn to be more fully man, though he still has far to go. The Nazi atrocities and those of the Assyrians did not both elicit the same resigned acceptance by public opinion. We need to make value judgements of human institutions: how do they let man become more fully man in steadily growing numbers? True monogamy is, from the conjugal point of view, humanly superior to polygamy.

There is, then, beyond vicissitudes, a line of progress; a humanizing meaning to history prolongs the meaning of evolution. It is up to us to make it an object of duty and to build a future serviceable to man.

Although there are automatic factors which push progress on, development in the economy, technical and cultural growth, and the rest, will not take place automatically. We shall not know "tomorrows that sing" of the noosphere, unless we work for them with lucidity.

Teilhard is no blind utopian lost in mists of the future. He very rightly, starting from the state of to-day, proposes that we have the will to go forward from it. Humanity's normal destiny in conformity with our nature, and therefore with our vocation, is the noosphere; but man has the power to act in an opposite sense and dehumanize himself. The co-creator can destroy creation. That is the risk God has taken.

Mankind's responsibility contains the chance of tragedy. Ignorance or sin is not merely prejudice or refusal to obey moral rules. They are against man's own well-being, his health, and those of others.

It is in this area that some speak of a Teilhardian

misunderstanding of sin. It is true that he was not content to give us catalog classifications. In agreement with St. Paul, he assures us that we are not constrained to submit to unexplained negative prohibitions of certain acts. We come under a positive morality, that of knowledge of the laws of our social personalization. It provides us with the dynamisms (virtues) necessary to its success while properly satisfying in the best way our real needs. It is a morality of yes, of vocation, of applying principles to concrete cases; it concentrates more on the obligation to rise and go forward than on accidental failures.

Everything should be judged in reference to what we are, that is, to what God expects of us. A human liberty which is both fragile from its origin and responsible—that is what makes history a way of the cross, a way which led the incarnation to culminate upon the cross.

History thus appears as the result of both the effort upward toward self-realization and the complaisant drifting which topples over into disorder. There is no opposition between individual morality and social morality. Rather, politics should be referred to criteria that affect man's progress; all men should find within society the possibility of fulfilling their capacities which, different as they are, are equal in complementarity, so that racism of any kind is plainly a grave error even from a scientific point of view.

History is the time-line of human progress. It becomes, under the weight of matter we have neglected to save (that is, to realize), the way of the cross of human suffering[3] upon which is written the way of the cross of the Creator who prohibited himself from any intervention other than that of coming to die in his turn on the cross.

[3] See Teilhard's discussion of the spiritual energy of suffering, *Oeuvres*, Vol. 7.

It is a way of the cross that began with the earliest men who, for all their ignorance and weakness, were free. In their immense pride, the pride of the ignorant and weak, they wanted only their own way, choosing because of their carnal origins the path of dehumanization which, although it was contrary to their nature, became for them as for us almost second nature.

Whoever considers human history and also knows man's capacity for good cannot but be convinced of the importance of this *original weakness* that makes it easier to fall than to rise through a *natural temptation to go against nature*, an aboriginal inadequacy for which we are not responsible but which leads us into acts for which we are responsible.

Contrary to some statements, Teilhard (though not expected to give us a theology of original sin) did attest to evidences of it over and over, showing them as an interdependent massive weight that called forth the solidarity of the redemption.

This original weakness will continue to exist, because man is man and it is not for us to dream of a coming golden age in which sin will disappear and it will be easy to be good. Even if the exploitation of man by man should disappear in the classless society of the future noosphere, it will always be hard to conquer temptation.

For the Christian responsible to God for the proper completion of creation, the drama is greater, in that sin is committed by one of Christ's members and in that perverseness in society affects the preparation on earth of what will be the city of God. He will always have the last word; but it is not the same for man, whether he has completed or failed to complete his task—that crucifying task which despite differences in perspective appears more and more to

be a *common value* requiring the collaboration of
believer and nonbeliever in the spirit of the man
who, after Teilhard, came and reminded us of the
conditions of good social growth, Pope John XXIII.

VIII
The Cross of Our Nature

Man rightly wants to find himself more and more free. In fact, he is less and less so, for he does not know what true human liberty is. Will woman be liberated because she has been given the false need of satisfying her erotic sensuality at any price, by permitting her to avoid impregnation technically? Are hypnotics, tranquilizers, sterilizing hormones really pills of freedom?

The real drama of man is his *human nature*. It is a much devaluated expression in this anti-metaphysical century in which there triumphs an anti-normative phenomenological philosophy. Teilhard, in the forefront of that normative science, human biology, has reminded us of the scientific demand for a return to an authentic metaphysics. Human biology is not the science of the body of man exclusive of his soul. It is the science of the whole body including the constituting presence of the soul, the science of the human being taken in his bodily and organic aspect, *bio-ontology* situating man as a floret of the animal series with an evolutionary rise in brain.

When the Church speaks of sexual morality and considers it her right to speak for non-Catholics as well as Catholics because she assumes the defense of the true values of human sexuality and conjugal union, no one understands. Non-believers and non-Catholics refuse to submit to her dogmas. Catholics find very hard, very much opposed to what they consider to be their natural needs, the laws of Catholic morality; obeying (without understanding them) their exterior restrictions, they risk either repressions or despairing falls, or rebellion and abandoning the sacraments. It is merely that, sad to say, no one any longer understands that plane of natural morality where the Catholic Church stands in the spirit of St. Paul: not demoralization, but an intrinsic morality which is superior hygiene, a factor difficult to maintain in equilibrium.

It is a matter of referral to human nature which will always require a difficult effort of lucidity and mastery of will. Unfortunately we make the will a kind of disembodied spiritual force that tries, without quite making it, to dull down if not to chastise flesh that is rebellious if not evil. The biological spirit underlying Teilhard's thought brings us indispensable objective insights on what the true and complete human nature and the human will are.

It is to conduct oneself within the unity (indissoluble here below) of body and spirit, so well described in St. Thomas Aquinas' metaphysics as a normal, healthy, adult (that is, educated) man, a truly civilized person, to employ fully the resources of mastery and reflection of our human higher brain.

It is a serious prejudice to believe what is natural for man lies in the easy unconstraint of what imitates the animal. Man is not an angel trying desperately to make a rebellious animal obey. He is neither angel nor animal. It is not possible to be natural in the human sense without a difficult asceticism. The drama is that the preachers of virtue have presented us with this asceticism in the guise of disembodied sanctity that holds the flesh in horror in a negative context of renunciation, mortification, dispossession, if not abjection. The fact is that asceticism is necessary in order to become a real man, not succumbing to the easy downgrade of natural temptations to self-degradation coming from hormones, complexes, needs, customs, habits, prejudices.

Faithfulness to human nature, the brain of man being what it is, demands incessant effort directed to humanization. That is what Teilhard proposes to us in his positive norm. Yet it is only humanization for the individual insofar as it is directed to the aid of others, for man is a social species that finds psychological equilibrium only in the balanced love of others. "You shall love your neighbor as yourself." is the psychobiological law of cerebral equilibrium.

Human effort, however, is not a nervous contraction performed to obey a law without understanding it. It is the psychotechnical art of being more of a man which demands above all, as the masters of yoga and Zen have well understood (though unfortunately in a context of depersonalizing metaphysics which has plainly denounced Teilhard), the lucid, calm and interior peace of one who has learned to use his brain to create calm within himself and so is able to assume fully the direction of his conduct, that is, of his cerebral control—following the very accurate expression of that benefactor of humanity who is still unfortunately so little known, the late Dr. Vittoz.

It is therefore necessary to revalorize the effort and so arrive at a just idea of what is truly natural and truly spontaneous, which is not letting go no matter what but is rather the acquisition of good habits and first of all of reflection and self-mastery.

Sexual morality is but one particular case of this.

Instead of struggling to have the Church change and accept, in the face of our inalterable needs which reveal that we are denatured through lack of education, a choice between contraceptive denaturalization of the sexual act or denaturalization of the person by sterilizing mutilation, provisionally through hormones or absolutely through surgery, let us work at promoting humanization of sexuality through education in self-mastery. It is in this sense that Teilhard addresses us. Contrary to the slanderous interpretation attributed to him by integrists ignorant of the "World and Life", he does not tell us that it is necessary to go toward sexual profligacy. It is on the contrary toward a reevaluation of the values of chastity and virginity that mankind must be orientated for its salvation. For possessive eroticism is the denial of that essential human intercourse between man and woman which is a factor in their complementary restoration of equilibrium where they mutually teach how to be more fully human, with the reconciliation between feminine sentimentalism and masculine rationalism accomplished on the level of true love which makes of them a synthesis. Education of adolescents in true chastity which is conjugal chastity, loving continence based on self-mastery which has been made a reflex and is the source of better spiritualizing carnal communion and of voluntary humanized procreation, the better understanding of priestly celibacy which is not a mutilation but a promotion on condition that it not be perverted by prejudices (puritanism, aloofness)—all these things go in the direction of humanization foreknown to Teilhard.

Man is only natural in the effort to rise and to help others rise but that effort has a concomitant relaxation. Thus we come to the synthesis of two seemingly opposite forms of self-comportment. Modern man insists on action and mastery of matter, the cosmos, the atom, life, the brain, the psychic structure. He is a son of Prometheus, rebelling against the gods, against nature.

The spirit of Christianity is, in contrast, one of abandon to providence, of acceptance. Some see conflict here. It is a grave error. The conflict is between possible deviations into voluntarism and sub-missiveness. What ought we to want? Not at all our fantasy of being free. The drama, the cross of our freedom, is that it lies in obedience to our nature, not the one we invent but the one we receive from our composition, whether we make of it a psycho-biological fact or see it as a call from God. Man is free only to be man, humanizing if not a dehumanizer, and it is not he who decides what it is to be man. To be man is not to master nature but to discover nature's laws so as to know their fullest possibilities. It is to renounce one's egotism in order to grow.

Therefore, far from finding the cross an unbearable restriction merely added on, we are enabled to en-counter it naturally. It is the impossibility, found by the man who wants to be a man, of abandoning himself to his strongest tendencies; it is his renunci-ation of their promptings out of fidelity to the human vocation inscribed in our psychobiological constitu-tion.

The difficulty of being a man inevitably suggests, since we are as we are, the need of a salvation to be given us freely by our Creator in his goodness. And that salvation has a model for us in the only "normal man" in history, our Lord Jesus who showed us that the greatest love lies in dying for and by the hand of those one loves. We want none of him. It is easy: crucify him, and the sacrifice of God is the pledge of our salvation.

IX
To Ripen
Is To Die

To understand that to be normal we must renounce our egotism, that to become more a person, a me, we must know how to be limited by others, is hard. We must fight the strong natural tendency to denaturalize ourselves that pushes us into endless greed—the greed of the rich, of the tyrant who does more harm than he knows not only to those he enslaves but to himself whom he has removed from the normal human condition. Teilhard said, "Whoever will passionately love Jesus hidden in the forces that exalt the earth, him will the earth maternally lift up in her giant arms; and she will cause him to contemplate the face of God."

That is not all. Remember the phrase, "Unless the seed die. . . ." It is in accord with the nature of living things that man is mortal, as it is in harmony with his nature to suffer. The biologist is ideally equipped to see the happy end-result of protective suffering and death which renew generations radically, thanks to sexuality, more radically than can simple unicellular division which, barring accidents, produces no corpses. That grief and death are in the real nature of mankind is the principal cross of our nature. Medico-fictional dreams of conquering death or grief will not alter it.

"If, my God, your kingdom were of this world, for me to lay hold of you it would suffice that I trust myself to the forces which make us suffer and die by making us grow visibly in ourselves or in that which is dearer than ourselves to us. But because the term toward which earth moves is beyond not only each individual thing but all things all together, because the work of the world consists not in itself engendering some supreme reality but in consuming itself through union with a preexisting Being, it appears that for man to reach the flaming center of the universe, it is not enough that he live more and more for himself nor that he spend his life in some earthly cause, however great. The world cannot finally rejoin you, Lord, other than by a kind of inversion, of turnabout, of excentric motion wherein not merely the success of individuals but also the very hint of any human advantage founders. For my being to be definitively joined to yours, there must die in me not just the monad but the mundane world; that is, I must pass through the shattering phase of a diminution nothing tangible appears to compensate. . . . With the increases this new day brings me, [I must receive] in my name and in the name of the world, labor, plain or hidden weakening, an increase in age and death that incessantly undermine the world for its salvation and its condemnation. . . . Whoever shall have passionately loved Jesus in the forces that make the earth die, him will the failing earth hold close in her giant arms, and with her he will wake again in the presence of God."

Teilhard in *The Divine Milieu* insisted particularly on these values of diminution, not simply those which by limiting us make us grow but those which truly

destroy us in our appearance here below. Man and
the world are mortal. The latter, despite the localized
rise in entropy of life, goes on toward its probable
extinction at least as far as the planet earth is con-
cerned, along with the solar system and perhaps
our whole galaxy. To love and cherish earth is to be
aware of this. Death lies at the heart of everything.

Of course, the believer knows that there is another
life and another world; but he is still a man. The
attitude of Teilhard at the end of *Comment je crois*
is most human. He had often said that he was not
afraid of death and that he was prepared to accept
the idea of his total disappearance. In his logical
reflections on science he had to admit, even before
coming to the level of true faith, the rational necessity
for personal survival, thus joining together metaphysics and revelation. Therefore, Teilhard knew that
death is nothing but a "change in state". And yet he
tells us, "After what I have just set forth as to my
conviction that there exists a personal divine term to
universal evolution, one might think that my future
life lies ahead of me serene and luminous. Death
would probably seem to me just like one of those
sleeps after which we never doubt we will see a
glorious morning dawn. Nothing could be further from
the truth. . . . To believe is not to see. As much as
anyone, I suppose, I walk among the shadows of
faith."

Nothing is more curious than the phenomenon
of aging; it consists of two opposite aspects. On one
side, it is incontestable that there is much that is negative: a progressive breakdown of the individual,
but one that will be better understood as medical
science learns to fight off the maladies of age. There
is also a positive side: a ripeness that increases the
value of the individual who is in decline. A like
ambiguity may be found at every stage of the vital

cycle. Only the egg at the moment of conception, with its prodigious power to expand, is totally young. To grow is from the very start to age and lose potential; but it is also to ripen and realize potential, while becoming more clearly differentiated. The contradiction between the two aspects of age is a mystery if one does not draw the logical conclusion, which confirms metaphysics and faith, that this being which declines while ripening is preparing for a metamorphosis which will bring it beyond flesh to another plane of being where it will keep its essential personality.

However, that other state of being remains a mystery, so much so that it is normal for the prospect of death, our own and that of those dear to us, to be painful to us. Teilhard thinks that only Christian faith in survival can give man the incentive to work. How can we work, if that work is ephemeral? If Teilhard takes so much trouble over this, it is precisely because he is convinced that mankind's salvation proceeds through reconciliation of apparently atheistic scientific humanism and Christian values. Shut off by individual and collective death, will not contemporary man be seized by disgust for life? The choice is, as he said, between death and adoration.

Though faith explains death's meaning, it does not thereby make it more pleasant. It is naturally difficult to accept on the human or the supernatural plane. We must disappear from this form that we love and our cherished world too is ephemeral. Teilhard often repeats that he is a son of earth; this earth, this matter, is not simply to be fought with as Jacob wrestled with the angel, in order that it be saved (rather than that we be lost with it); we must accept that it is a provisional state. We are not exiled on earth for expiation but delegated to earth which is not the finished land, so we may prepare for its

final transformation by God under the leadership of
the "Son of Man".

In the face of death, let us not make our faith the
pretext for a stoicism as inhuman as that of some
non-believers. Let us rather imitate our Lord who
performed his greatest miracles in fighting against
death, as when death had brought despair to a mother
or father, or when his friend Lazarus died. And yet
he well knew that it is not in so restricted a sense that
he was the true conquerer of death.

That a natural act should be so painful is strange.
Dogma offers us an explanation: man in God's plan
was intended to die, certainly, but so as to pass into
another state in the peace, harmony and balance of
the Virgin on her day of assumption. It is the un-
balance due to the sin of poor mastery of the flesh
that broke everything off. We must now learn how
to fall asleep happy in the peace of the Lord, like one
of the heroes of Aldous Huxley's *Island* practicing
the yoga of death or like a civilized woman terrified
by the natural phenomenon of childbirth who must
learn to use her mind to master this natural function
and so bring forth her child in joy.

X
We Go
Toward Fire

A n almost total misunderstanding of Teilhard's sci-
entifico-Christian vision is displayed by those who
see in it a form of easy naturalism. His vision, as we
have noted, takes sin into account; it further sees our
individual salvation as dependent on the difficult
effort of individual and collective humanization. Yet
he never hints that man might through his own
strength be about to construct the heavenly Jerusalem
which God would come down to inhabit. For one
thing, we have seen that man's strength consists in
putting himself at the service of a task imposed on
him by his nature and by nature itself, a task for which
he receives God's grace, whether he knows it or not.
Then too, Teilhard does not guarantee us an inevitable success; success depends on free human choice.
We have seen that he specifically allows for the possibility of failure should man despair; but failure
might also result from ignorance, ending up in radio-
active destruction perhaps or in imprudent bank-
ruptcy of natural resources or in a social form that
would inflict totalitarian depersonalization on man.

It would therefore be a mistake to think Teilhard's

vision contrary to traditional Christian views. The human individual does not go with perfect assurance toward eternal happiness, because he does not know who he is, nor does he know if he stands within God's love or in separation from it. It is at death that the nature he has given himself through his life will bring with it a different reaction. Death thrusts us into love and love is fire. We shall be burned. Burned with love if we are of the right fuel—and we shall burn in the glory of heaven. Burned with suffering, desperately, if we are bad in what we have made of our nature—and that is hell. Burned with a purifying suffering—and that is the rise toward heaven, purgatory. It is nothing other than being plunged into love.

As for the path of humanity in building up the human city, Teilhard does not see it as going anywhere but into the Apocalypse. It is too simple to set St. John and Teilhard in opposition. Will all be destroyed in a frightful cataclysm? We have no idea. It is to slip into a falsified harmony to claim that St. John meticulously depicts a final atomic war.

St. John, the apostle of love, and Teilhard, the scientific prophet of love, did have comparable visions. It matters little what the details are. They foresee that (just as on the individual plane) the human accomplishment will be destroyed to the extent that it is bad, where man has ill performed his task of amorization, and God will resume everything on new bases. To the extent that it is good, too, it is destined to be destroyed. It will be burned in confronting the fire. It is certainly this work which will be glorified and the human task is its preparation; but in the change of state it will nonetheless pass through a glorifying combustion.[4]

[4] "The better the leaves, the better leaf-mould they make," said a Marxist martyr. Rather, the better glory they make.

In viewing the rise of complexification, Teilhard does not mention only the thresholds of the step up into life, and of the step up into reflection. He also envisages, at the far limit of science and illuminated by faith, a threshold yet more extraordinary: the threshold of glorification, at the meeting when the story is ended of the convergence of world and man, with Omega point who is God in Christ.

In a way, there are two aspects to Omega point. First it is the ideal state of the noosphere in its natural aspect which the non-believing evolutionist Julian Huxley has also perceived. Then there is Teilhard's analysis of Omega point made outside of all theology, and which leads him to give it the attributes of God and to identify it with God in Christ. The meeting with Omega point is thus the *point of Parousia.*

In his reflections on thermodynamics, Teilhard insists on the contradiction between the waste expenditure of energy and growth localized by life. In the world there is something that rises while everything falls into disrepair. For him, what rises does not go toward its cut-off point but draws close to a change of state, a kind of *reflection of energy.*

Still more than for the step up into life which implied a kind of creative action intensified so as to appear in the surcomplexification of matter; still more than for the step up into reflection, during which matter once again surcomplexified exhibited through the human brain certain powers that had no basis of common measure with it (thereby indicating the true spiritual and therefore indestructible nature of the human "form")—when it is a matter of this supreme threshold, there is a new relationship of the Uncreated and the created into which the former places itself in a more important way.

"Whenever the end of the world is mentioned an immediate thought of misery comes to mind. . . . Cosmic catastrophe, biological disintegration, or simply growth halted and age advancing, pessimistic representations of earth's last days have in common that they attribute without correction to all of life the characteristics and attributes of our individual and rudimentary ends. Rupture, disease, decreptitude. Such is the death of man, such the death of mankind. . . .

"Not a halt at all, in any form whatsoever, but a last progression coming in its biological hour. A ripening, and a paroxysm. When by the sufficient buildup of a sufficient number of elements this motion, which is essentially convergent by nature, will have reached such an intensity and such a quality that to further unify itself humanity ought to . . . reflect itself in its turn 'punctually' (that is, in this instance, to abandon its organo-planetary support in order to excentrate itself upon the transcendent center of its increasing concentration), then that will be for the spirit of earth the end and the crowning moment.

"The end of the world: massive interior return upon itself of a noosphere that has come simultaneously to the extreme limits of its complexity and its concentration. The end of the world: balance turned upside down, detaching the finally completed spirit from its material matrix so that its full weight rests at last upon God-Omega. The end of the world: critical point of both emergence and emersion, of ripeness and escape."

Glorious, natural, supernatural destiny of a crucifying, crucified world. Final sacrifice wherein matter abandons its laws and its weight and keeps only its essence, a sacrifice that, like a vocation, is not fulfilled without pain.

Yet does not the eucharist give us the right image for it, when bread and wine subsist no longer except as accidental appearances? Teilhard is well known for having used the analogy very frequently without falling into confusion. After the offering of matter and of technique in his "Mass upon the world" of a priest-scientist, he presents them to Fire which is above the world, and it becomes an Apocalypse:

"It is done. Fire has once more penetrated earth. . . . With no quaking, without thunder the flame has illuminated everything from within. From the heart of the least atom to the energy of the most universal laws, it has so naturally invaded, individually and all at once, each element, each spring, each link of our cosmos that one might believe it spontaneously afire."

But, Teilhard adds, giving the sacrifice its full meaning, "If Fire be come down into the heart of the world, it is ultimately come to take me and absorb me. From that moment, it is not enough that I contemplate it and with a sustained faith ceaselessly intensify its ardor around me. After having cooperated with all my strength in the consecration that causes it to leap forth, I must consent at last to that communion which will give it, in my person, the food it ultimately came to seek." No communion which is not crucifying. In union with Christ the Christian is the maker of his own progress on this earth, but he is thenceforth on the slope of the resurrection—dead and resurrected with Christ, St. Paul tells us.

XI
Will Everything
Be Saved?

The legends of a false Teilhardism, opposed to Teilhard's real thought, give an important place to the notion that there is no room for the Christian thesis of hell in the thought of Teilhard. Nothing could be further from the truth.

What did he say in *The Phenomenon of Man*, not in the appendix where, out of concern lest he be misunderstood, Teilhard returns in detail to the problem of evil, but in his conclusion on the end of the world?

There are two possible solutions. One is optimistic: we are going toward a minimum of evil. The final convergence will be worked out in peace though not without extreme tension. "Such a result, certainly, would conform most harmoniously with the theory."

"But it is also possible that, following a law nothing in the past has yet evaded, evil, growing at the same time as good, should at last reach its paroxysm also in a specifically new manner. No heights without depths. . . . For a last time, ramification again. In this second hypothesis, which conforms more closely to the traditional Apocalyptic ones, perhaps three curves would continue to rise together toward the future: unavoidable reduction of the organic possibilities of earth; internal schism of consciousness always more divided between two opposed ideals of evolution; positive attraction of the center of centers in the heart of those who will turn themselves toward it. And earth will end at the triple point where, quite in conformity with the ways of life, these three curves will meet and simultaneously attain their maximum.

"Death of the planet, materially exhausted; the noosphere torn in two over what form its unity should assume; and simultaneously, giving all its meaning and its value to the event, liberation of that portion of the universe which will have succeeded, through time, space and evil, in laboriously synthesizing itself to the end.

"Not an indefinitely continued progress—a hypothesis the convergent nature of noogenesis contradicts —but an ecstasy, out beyond the dimensions and borders of the visible universe. Ecstasy in concord or in discord but, in either case, because of an inner excess of tension. The only biological conclusion suited to and imaginable for the phenomenon of man."

And in *The Divine Milieu:* "We have never ceased to feel at our backs the dark emptiness—the rarefaction or the absence of God upon which our course remained suspended. But these lower shadows that we try to flee could just as well have been a kind of abyss opening out into nothingness. Imperfection, evil, sin, the flesh, these were above all regressive in meaning, a reverse side of things that ceased to exist for us to the extent that we thrust ourselves deeper into God. Your Revelation, Lord, obliges me to believe more fully. The powers of evil in the universe are not only an attraction, a deviation, a subtraction sign, an annihilating return to plurality. In the course of the world's spiritual evolution, conscious elements, Monads, have freely detached themselves from the mass that your attraction draws. Evil became as if incarnate in them, substantialized in them. And there are now around me, mingling with your luminous presence, dim presences, evil beings,[5] malignant things. And this separated group represents an irreversible and immortal waste in the genesis of the world. There are darknesses which are not only lower but exterior. That is what the New Testament tells us.

"My God, among all the mysteries in which we are to believe, there is doubtless no other which so much affronts our human views. You have told me, my God, to believe in hell. Yet you have forbidden me to think with absolute certitude of a single man that he is damned. So I shall not try here to look at the damned—or even, in a way, to know if there are any. But accepting hell on your word, as a structural element of the universe, I shall pray, I shall meditate, until out of this formidable thing its complement dawns on me, strengthening and beatifying even to the views that you have opened for me upon your omnipresence. . . .

"Is it necessary to look hard to discover in the exterior darkness an increase of tension and a deepening of your greatness? Considered in their malignant voluntary action, the powers of evil are in no way able to trouble the atmosphere of the divine milieu; this I already know. To the extent that they seek to penetrate my universe, their influence (if I have enough faith) undergoes the common lot of all created energy; seized, twisted by your irresistible energy, temptations and disorders are converted to

[5] In *L'Etre humain selon Teilhard* I have shown the possible role of a devolutionary Satan and of coevolutionary angels.

good and inflame the brazier of love. . . . The
damned is not excluded from the pleroma but from
its luminous side and its beatification. He loses it, but
it is not lost for him. . . . Therefore hell does not
destroy anything by existing. . . . The summit is only
measured properly by the chasm that crowns it. . . .
Does not the reality of this negative pole of the world
double the urgency and the immensity of the power
with which you build on me? . . . I want to include
in my habitual and practical view of the world the
constantly menacing gravity of condemnation—not so
much to fear you, Jesus, as to be more passionately on
your side. . . . Now clothed in the tremendous
power of selection which puts you at the summit of
the world as the universal principle of attraction and
of repulsion, you truly appear to me as the immense
and living force that I looked for everywhere so that
I might adore. The fires of heaven and the fires of hell
are not two different forces but contrary manifestations of the same energy.

"May the flames of hell not reach me, Master, nor
any of these I love. . . . May they not reach anyone,
my God (you will forgive me this senseless prayer,
I know). But for each of us may their somber rays
be added, along with all the chasms they make dis-
cernible, to the burning fullness of the divine
milieu."

Finally let us take the third mystical meditation of
Le Christ dans la matière, which is called, "The Monstrance". After the host, grown gigantically, has in-
corporated all the values of the world, we see how
its withdrawal into the monstrance admits of a left-
out remainder:

"When the flood lowers, or the flame falls back,
brilliant splashes and stains of fire mark the air that
was briefly invaded by the sea or the blaze. Then too,
as the host closed over upon itself, as a flower closes

up its calix, some refractory elements of the universe stayed behind it in the exterior shadows. Something still made them luminous; but it was a spirit of perverted, corrosive and poisonous light. These elements burned like torches or glowed like braziers."

After that, who can claim that Teilhardian optimism ignores the depth and dimension of evil? And these texts are moreover published; all the commentators have read them. Must one conclude, therefore, that for them what counts is not what Teilhard wrote or thought but what he ought to have thought and written to conform to their notion of him?

XII

A Normally
Difficult Faith

Some, faced with the great Teilhardian synthesis,
reproach him less with intrinsic optimism than
with the fact that his unification of faith and science
seems too easy. It is basically the highest praise of
Teilhard, for this apparent facility was the result of
the painful and crucifying work of his entire life. How
much easier it would have been for him to divide his
life in two—as, on the one hand, a good paleontologist
like the rest and, on the other, an excellent Jesuit
priest. He would have scandalized no scientists by
being a believer within the context of science, nor any
Catholics by integrating faith with an apparent scientific materialism that some use to try to destroy him.
But such an unnatural separation had no part in his
vocation of priest-scientist.

At the start he had two loves, his science of tran-
sient matter and his faith in the Christian absolute. It
took all his life, even with the intuitions of the war
years, 1914-18, for him to elaborate a unified vision
wherein God and Christ appear at the heart of matter.

The task was hard because it was no mere idealistic
conceptual elaboration but faithfulness to a double

reality, the reality of science and the reality of faith, in a synthesis that wholly engaged him. This is not the place to analyze the stages of that great vision Teilhard forged for himself, which he offers us as the basis of our own reflections and personal efforts.[6]

Despite the objectivity of his scientific start, Teilhard proposes it to us as a faith: *Comment je crois (How I Believe)* is his essay which does not give a theological point of view but in which he first, prolonging and going beyond science, bids us reflect on the implications of science, bringing us up to the threshold of religious belief, before going on to question religions in order to show that an authentic Christianity best agrees with science, for it is the religion which gives matter its fullest meaning, its greatness as well as its weakness.

A faith is very much more than an area of knowledge: one enters wholly into engagement with it with one's most intimate convictions; it goes beyond the limited stages of sentimentality or rationality toward the total understanding which is of the order of the heart—though not in the least contrary to reason therefore. Surely it was with all his heart that the evolutionist, Teilhard, looked as a scientist at the universe charged with love as it had evolved to terminate in the full reality of man. One might well cherish it.

But faith is also less than knowledge. If, as Teilhard says, to believe is to make an act of synthesis, that includes an element of subjectivity that is not found to the same degree in strictly analytic knowledge which is less personally significant for us.

And it is here that a painful aspect of Teilhard's thought lies. He considers that the salvation of man-

[6] See my schema in *La pensée scientifique de Teilhard.*

kind and the modern world depends on this junction
of earthly values and Christian values. He lived out
that synthesis himself. He is the living bridge between two hostile milieux which do not know each
other, but in both of which he is at home: science
and the Church. But there is no traffic over this
bridge which is a cross, like that of Claudel's Jesuit
between two worlds. Scientists are either materialists or careful to keep faith and science separate;
believers do not trust science which may be sus-
pected of endangering faith.

Father Leroy has told us of Father Teilhard's
anguish from time to time, because he was unable to
make himself understood. It was not for the reason
the Marxist Kahane supposed, in thinking he was
troubled by doubts about his own synthesis. It was
plain that he was astonished to find himself the
only one able to see what he found self-evident, and
that he could not engage philosophers and theologians
in fruitful discussion.

Yet here again, Teilhard's realistic optimism won
out. What matter his distress—one day others would
see! His problem was that of one ahead of his time.
"It suffices for truth to appear one single time within
one single mind, for it to then withstand whatever
would try to prevent it from invading everywhere
and inflaming everything."

Just as it was not necessary to remind Teilhard of
the horrors in nature and in history, so it was unnecessary to protest to him that belief is difficult. He
would have readily accepted the correct theses of
Father Roqueplo [7] on "a normally difficult faith"
which are especially interesting to scientists and
the steadily growing number of those influenced by
today's world which is dominated by a scientific

[7] In *Science et Foi*. Fayard.

attitude. Father Oew converted a dock worker by showing him the beauty of living matter. That is logical, but its logic is not apparent to most scientists for whom scientific method is the opium that cuts them off entirely from the whole field of metaphysical explanation through which it is possible to give a complete religious and Christian meaning to science's apparent materialism.

Nor were scientists the only ones to grieve Teilhard. What is there to say of the Marxists, passionately earthbound, who persist in dehumanizing us under heavens set too low; or of the existentialists who see only the absurd; or of the Thomists boxed up in their concepts and cut off from that reality which Thomas Aquinas so well explained; or of the contemporary philosophers and their phenomenology that rejects any ideas of essence and nature. In addition, among scientists it is not only the subject of faith that is hard to discuss: physicists reject the inwardness of things and the Teilhardian view of energy by calling Teilhard a bad philosopher or poet; sociologists accuse him of confusing history and natural history. Capping the list of ways in which Teilhard was misunderstood, is the fact that he was not even permitted to express himself freely because there were those who thought him dangerous.

These privations likewise found a place in the Teilhardian vision. Whether it be due to nature or because excess rising from original sin is added to nature (which is, as we have observed, no contradiction) in essential respects we are disabled. We have already recalled the evidence given by Teilhard who, although having rational certitude, still lived in the shadows of faith since believing and seeing are not the same thing.

"The shadows of faith," he said. "To justify those shadows, so strangely incompatible with the divine sun, the doctors have given the explanation that the Lord chooses to hide himself in order to prove our love. It would be necessary to be incurably absorbed in thought as a game (*jeux d'esprit*) and to have never met in oneself or others the suffering of doubt, in order to see nothing hateful in this solution.

"What, Lord? Would you allow your creatures to go lost, anguished and calling for help, needing you to show one ray of your glance, just the hem of your garment, for them to come running to you—and you would refuse it to them?

"The obscurity of faith is, to my mind, just a particular instance of the problem of evil. And to rise above its deathly scandal, I see only one way: it is to recognize that if God lets us suffer, sin, doubt, it is that he is not now able to cure us and show us himself all at once. And if he is not now able, it is simply because we are still incapable, because of the stage our universe is at, of greater organization and of more light. For a creation, in the course of developing itself in time, disorder is inevitable. Here again the liberating solution is given to us by evolution.

"No, God does not hide himself, I am certain, so that we may seek him, anymore than he lets us suffer to increase our merit. Quite the contrary; bending over creation which is rising toward him, he works with all his strength to beatify and to illuminate it. He watches over his new-born like a mother. But our eyes are not yet able to perceive him. Will it not take the full length of the centuries for our eyes to open to the light?

"Our doubts like our disorders are the price and the very condition of a universal achievement. Under these conditions, I agree to go forward to the end on a road of which I am more and more certain, toward horizons more and more drowned in mist."

XIII
Teilhard Crucified

The lack of understanding Teilhard has encountered since his death has been widespread. It has come from groups as different as the integrists of Action Fatima, Charbonneau who is Manichean, some Thomists boxed off from science and closed to the wise explanations of Daujat or Grenet, Domenach and the group at *Esprit* who fail to grasp the relationship between his personalism and that of Mounier, Marxists who reject his biologism and call his faith a "superstructure" while yet showing some sympathy for his thought, etc. It is a lack of understanding that simply deepens the lack he experienced throughout his career.

Was Teilhard an optimist who ignored the cross? To think so would take insensitivity or masochism, for he was crucified all his life for having wanted to be an apostle of the Church in the modern world.

The facts are well known and no one denies their double aspect. They were beneficent in that they opened Teilhard's thought to include the world's full dimensions in sending him toward the region where Sinanthropus still lay hidden, and in making possible his meeting with American scientific circles toward the end of his life. But there was also the cruel aspect that consisted in sending off to the other end of the world a man who it was feared would convert atheists and endanger ill-taught believers, in forbidding the honor done the Church in the offer of a Collège de France chair to a Jesuit, in sending far away from his beloved Paris a sick and aging man who had just returned there.

Others might have vacillated in their faith or loyalty. With Teilhard nothing of the sort ever happened. The admirable exchange of letters between him and the General of his order, published by Father Leroy, is public knowledge.

A fine article that deserves to be widely read was written by Father Barjon in the Carmelite magazine, *Foi vivante,* on the Christian and religious loyalty of Father Teilhard (*Foi vivante,* N. 15; it was followed in N. 18 by an article by M. Madaule on Teilhard and the love of neighbor, replying as was proper to the calumnies of Charbonneau and Tresmontant). "One must have read the retreat notes written every year by Father Teilhard to realize what scruples his soul remained capable of; some, because of the faith whose optimism shines out from all his work, run the risk of minimizing his very acute moral sensitivity and the anguish to which it was roused at the danger of letting itself be trapped into pride or sin."

One day, someone should bring together the varied testimony that will improve our view of Teilhard the priest—not just the mystic of the Mass upon the altar of the world, the prophet, but also the guide, the spiritual counselor who knew how to show each person the greatest understanding and the greatest sympathy, of course by showing the truth, but particularly by starting from the other's point of view and knowing how to find some part of the truth everywhere. It might be that all the time he lost in help-

ing those Providence sent him was also a cross to
bear, but he knew such a cross was part of his vocation and part of his recompense too. For if great
teachers condemned him with stupifying lack of understanding, there were many ordinary unremarkable
people who found the happiness of the Lord's company, thanks to him.

Barjon goes on to say, "His great suffering when
faced with the demands of obedience lay far less in
his mortification, however cruel, as a man of letters
or as a thinker under restrictions laid down to limit
the expression of his thought, than it did in the ter-
rible inner drama of conscience sprung from meeting
with the opposition of his superiors. Any generous
attitude must have, at the same time, its somber side.

"When he had to leave the Institut Catholique and
Paris because someone denounced him by sending
Rome one of his reflections on original sin that had
been intended to enlighten a non-believer, and which
was taken for a voicing of a new dogma, he wrote,
'I cut a good enough figure, but within, it is something
that resembles agony and storm.'

"Yet in the violent disturbance he experienced, his
religious faith was never shaken for an instant. He
never for an instant thought of creating a stir, any
more than it occurred to him to leave the Company.
But he was still anguished by the act of obedience
required of him. Was it an act compatible with the
no less certain obligation he had to bear witness?
Wasn't there a kind of cowardice in submitting? He
could not make it out clearly, and explained himself
to Father Valensin:

" 'I think I see that if I were to withdraw myself
(or get my back up in any way at all; humanly it
would be so easy and so pleasant), I would be un-
faithful to my faith in our Lord's animation of all the
events in the world and in the full meaning he has,

higher than that of all the world's components. I'd compromise the worth of my ideas, besides, among our own if not in others' eyes. It is essential for me to show by example that if my ideas seem to innovate they do make me as faithful as anyone to the ancient attitude. That is what I think I see, but even there, there are shadows. Oh, friend, tell me I am not disobedient to my ideal by being obedient.'"

That last shattering phrase sums up the whole problem. As soon as he had received his correspondent's reply, Father Teilhard again carefully set out his difficulties: "You have answered me, as you know well, in the way I know I shall take, with the help of God. But what I should like is to have that strength and also that profound joy that are to be drawn from the certainty that one is doing what is best. I say it over again to you: my fear (the one that causes my deepest uneasiness) is that in giving in, I go toward the *tutius* and not the *verius;* it is that to take the usual broad path under cover of loyalty might only be lack of courage. I hope I'll be, with our Lord's help, as 'decent' as you'd want. I'm just referring to you a difficulty of my mind, my wits, that is keeping me from acting in the fullness of peace. I believe that I shall take communion with profound joy from this little chalice; but at least let me be sure that it is the blood of Christ."

Publication of his World War I letters has further shown us it was from then on that Teilhard realized the essential message he bore could not pass freely, and that this would be the drama of his life.

It is a drama that is still going on. Leaving for Rome in 1948, Teilhard declared, "I am going to say there what is in my heart, but not what weighs on my heart. . . . For nothing weighs on my heart at all; I bear no one any grudge."

Barjon continues, "So while his life lasted Father

Teilhard with total loyalty, without trying to protect himself from assault, went on consenting to every sacrifice that was asked of him."

Every one, indeed. Yet if he was persecuted, he was also protected and he was never prevented from diffusing his ideas in clandestine ways. As Barjon says, "One may perceive the demands nothing could confuse, made by his apostle's heart. He took up the words of St. Paul, 'Woe to me if I do not teach the Good News.' He never wrote anything except for others. His thought, it seemed to him, did not belong to him; indeed it had taken shape thanks to others too. It remained the property of those for whom it had ripened and flashed forth, in the shape of evidence. . . .

"The decisive reason for Father Teilhard's conduct in saving his writings and confiding them to others before his death was the conviction that he could not consent to the burial of documents with limits and possible dangers that he certainly understood, but which he thought the men of his time needed more than ever."

One cross more, in the ambiguity of this world: he who brings back the lost sheep scandalizes the faithful sheep. Which to choose? To strengthen the faithful sheep—that is the marvelous answer given by Vatican Council II, of which Teilhard could not know he was the forerunner.

"We may conclude by saying," Father Barjon testifies, "that it was the essential love of God and of God alone that sufficed to preserve the unity and maintain the fundamental loyalty of this profoundly religious soul though it was torn by contradictory demands."

May we not also say of him what he said of his sister Marguerite, that he had "silently metamorphosed into light the worst shadows of the world", thanks to "the astonishing Christian revelation of a suffering transformable (so long as it has been accepted well) into an expression of love and a principle of union", that "prodigious spiritual generator of energy, born of the cross"?